Impressum
Verlag: BABADADA GmbH, Nedderfeld 112 , 22529 Hamburg
Geschäftsführer / Verlagsleitung: Harald Hof
Druck: Books on Demand GmbH, In de Tarpen 42, 22848 Norderstedt

Imprint
Publisher: BABADADA GmbH, Nedderfeld 112 , 22529 Hamburg, Germany
Managing Director / Publishing direction: Harald Hof
Print: Books on Demand GmbH, In de Tarpen 42, 22848 Norderstedt

lekol

school

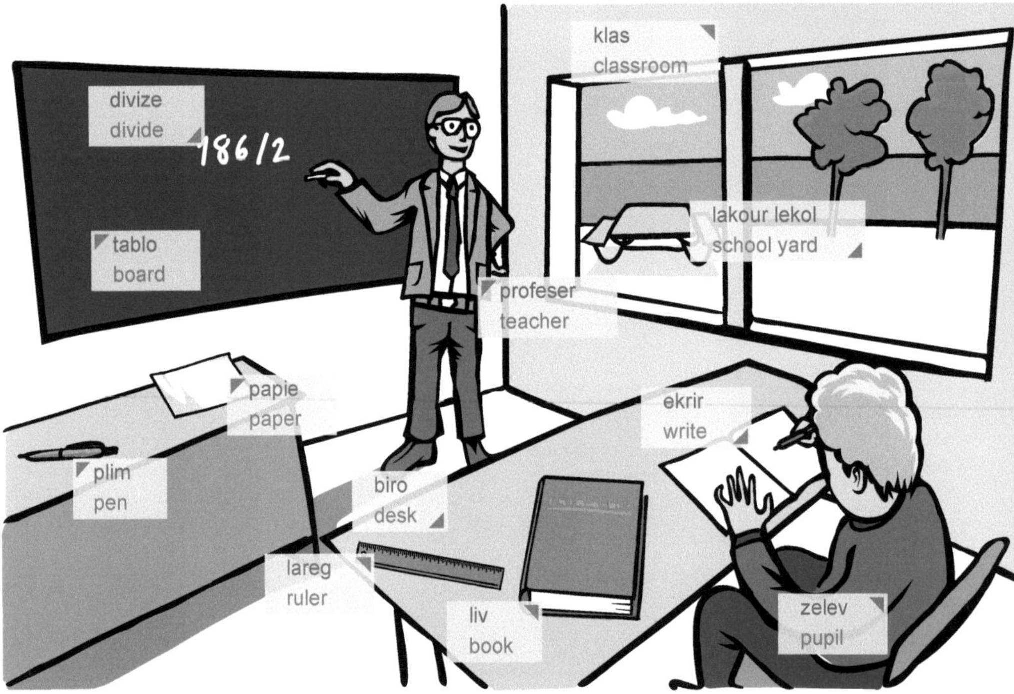
klas
classroom
divize
divide
186/2
tablo
board
lakour lekol
school yard
profeser
teacher
papie
paper
ekrir
write
plim
pen
biro
desk
lareg
ruler
liv
book
zelev
pupil

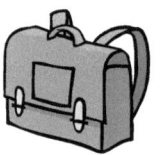

sak lekol

satchel

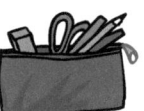

plimie

pencil case

kreyon

pencil

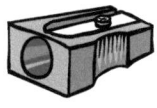

egizwar

pencil sharpener

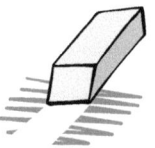

gom

rubber

kaye desin

drawing pad

desin

drawing

pinso

paintbrush

bwat lapintir

paint box

sizo

scissors

lakol

glue

kaye devwar

exercise book

devwar

homework

nimero

number

2+2

azoute

add

5-2

retire

subtract

2×2

miltipliye

multiply

kalkile

calculate

A

let

letter

ABCDEFG
HIJKLMN
OPQRSTU
VWXYZ

alfabet

alphabet

mo

word

text

text

lir

read

lakre

chalk

leson

lesson

rezis

register

lexame

examination

sertifika

certificate

iniform lekol

school uniform

ledikasion

education

lansiklopedi

encyclopedia

liniversite

university

mikroskop

microscope

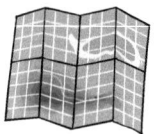

map

map

poubel

waste-paper basket

vwayaz
travel

lotel
hotel
Grand
loberz
hostel
ROOMS
EXCHANGE
biro sanz
currency exchange office
valiz
suitcase
loto
car

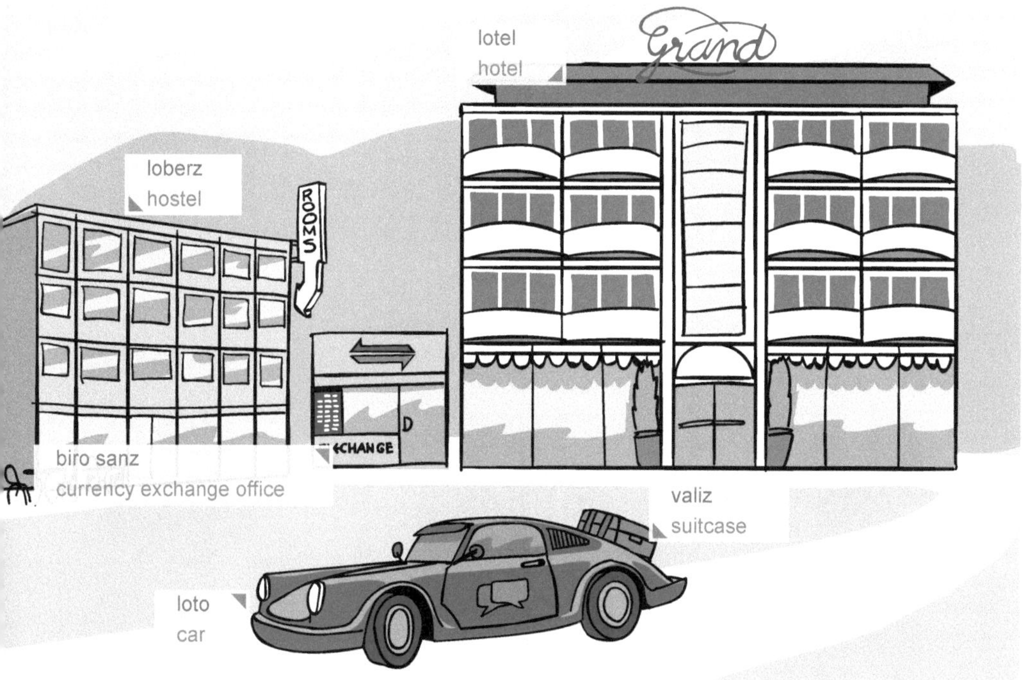

langaz

language

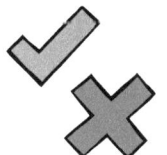

wi / non

yes / no

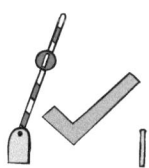

okay

Okay

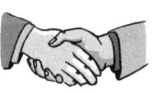

Alo

hello

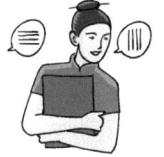

tradikter

translator

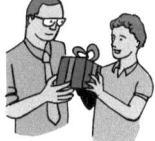

Mersi

Thank you

komie sa..?
how much is…?

Mo pa pe konpran
I don´t get it

problem
problem

Bonswar!
Good evening!

Bonzour!
Good morning!

Bonn nwi!
Good night!

o-revwar
goodbye

direksion
direction

bagaz
luggage

sak
bag

sak-a-do
backpack

ot
guest

pies
room

sak kousaz
sleeping bag

latant
tent

lofis tourism

tourist information

laplaz

beach

kart kredi

credit card

ti-dezene

breakfast

dezene

lunch

dine

dinner

biye

Ticket

lasanser

elevator

tem

stamp

frontier

border

ladwann

customs

lanbasad

embassy

viza

visa

paspor

passport

transpor
transport

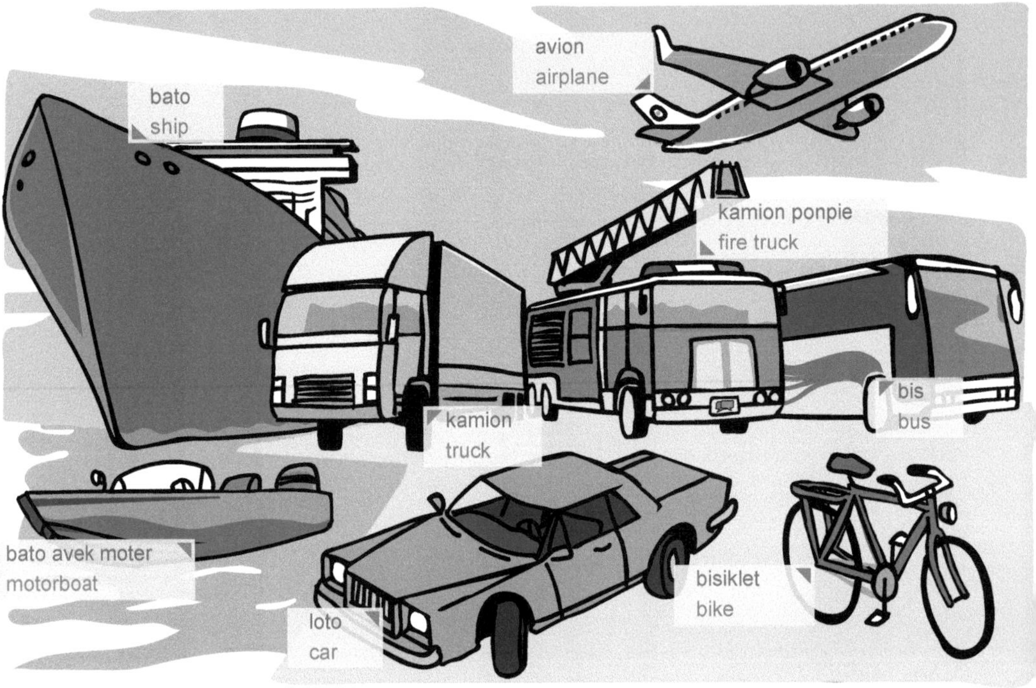
avion
airplane
bato
ship
kamion ponpie
fire truck
bis
bus
kamion
truck
bato avek moter
motorboat
bisiklet
bike
loto
car

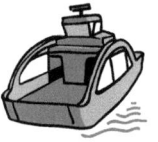

feri
ferry

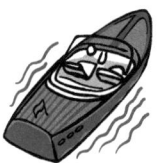

bato
boat

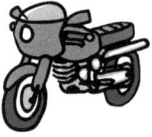

motosiklet
motorbike

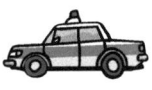

loto lapolis
police car

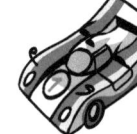

loto lekours
racing car

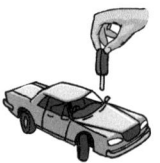

loto lokasion
rental car

ko-vwatiraz

car sharing

kamion towing

tow truck

kamion salte

garbage truck

moter

engine

lesans

fuel

filing

fuel station

pano indikasion

traffic sign

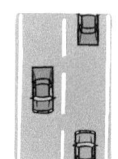

trafik

traffic

anbouteyaz

traffic jam

parking

parking lot

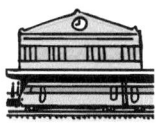

stasion trin

train station

ray

tracks

trin

train

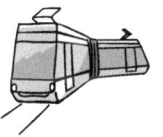

tram

tram

vagon

wagon

elikopter

helicopter

aeropor

airport

towing

tower

pasaze

passenger

kontener

container

karton

carton

sario

cart

panie

basket

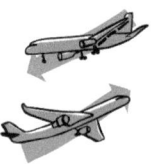

dekole / aterir

take off / land

lavil

city

vilaz

village

sant-vil

city center

lakaz

house

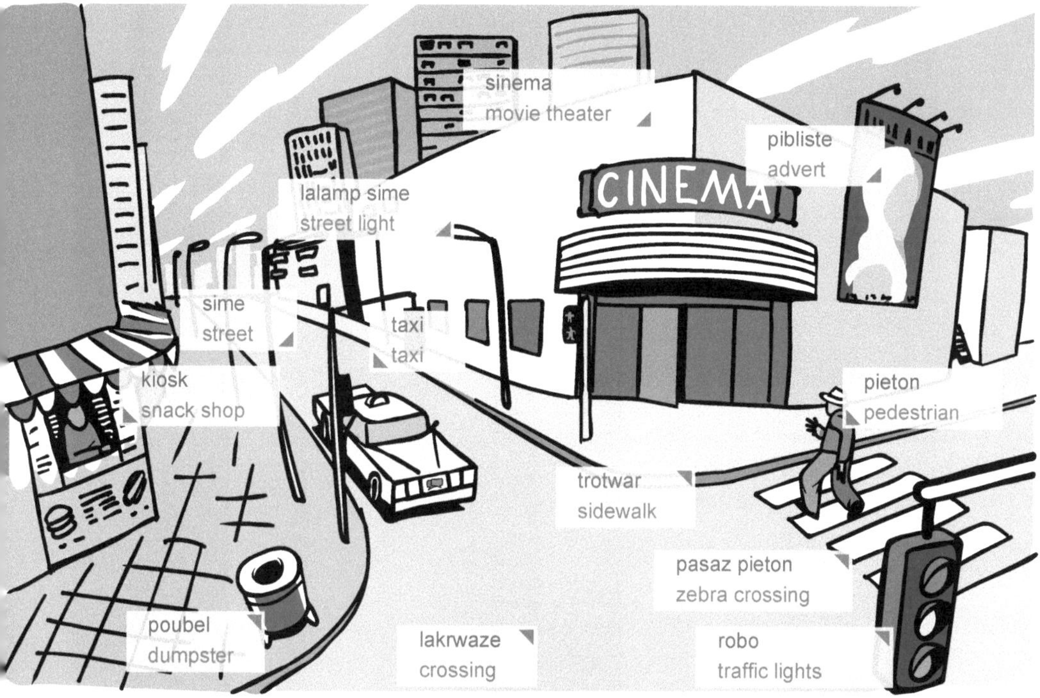

CINEMA

sinema — movie theater

pibliste — advert

lalamp sime — street light

sime — street

taxi — taxi

kiosk — snack shop

pieton — pedestrian

trotwar — sidewalk

pasaz pieton — zebra crossing

poubel — dumpster

lakrwaze — crossing

robo — traffic lights

kabann
hut

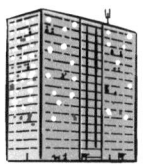

flat
apartment

stasion trin
train station

minisipalite
city hall

mize
museum

lekol
school

liniversite

university

labank

bank

lopital

hospital

lotel

hotel

farmasi

pharmacy

biro

office

libreri

book shop

magazin

shop

fleris

flower shop

sipermarse

supermarket

bazar

market

gran magazin

department store

pwasonnri

fishmonger's shop

sant komersial

mall

lepor

harbor

park

park

labank

bench

pon

bridge

leskalie

stairs

metro

subway

tinel

tunnel

bistop

bus stop

bar

bar

restoran

restaurant

bwat-a-let

postbox

pano

street sign

parkmet

parking meter

zoo

zoo

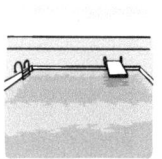

pisinn

swimming pool

moske

mosque

laferm

farm

polision

pollution

simitier

cemetery

legliz

church

lespas pou zwe

playground

tanp

temple

peizaz

landscape

fey
leaf

pano indikasion
signpost

sime
path

preri
meadow

ros
stone

randonner
hiker

pie
tree

larivier
river

lerb
grass

fler
flower

lavale

valley

kolinn

hill

lak

lake

bwa

forest

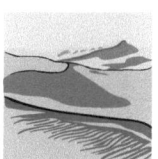

dezer

desert

volkan

volcano

sato

castle

larkansiel

rainbow

sanpinion

mushroom

palmie

palm tree

moutik

mosquito

mous

fly

fourmi

ant

abey

bee

zarenie

spider

koksinel

beetle

grenouy

frog

ekirey

squirrel

erison

hedgehog

lapin

hare

ibou

owl

zwazo

bird

sign

swan

sangliye

boar

serf

deer

elan

moose

dam

dam

eolienn

wind turbine

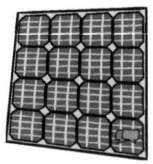

pano soler

solar panel

klima

climate

restoran
restaurant

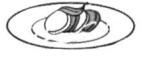

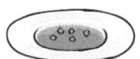

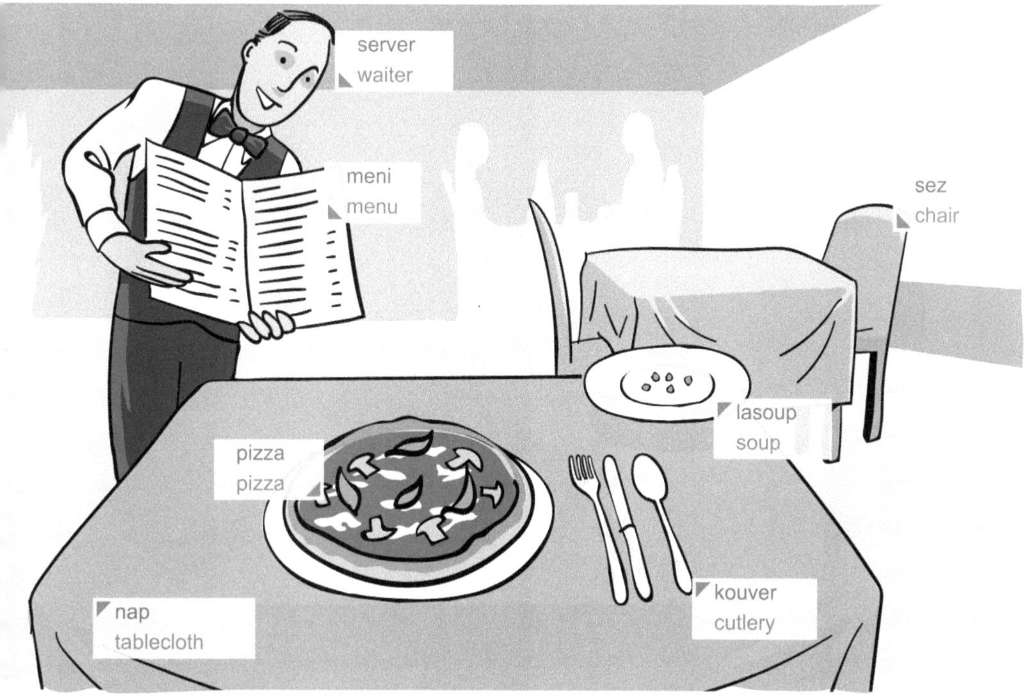
server
waiter
meni
menu
sez
chair
lasoup
soup
pizza
pizza
kouver
cutlery
nap
tablecloth

lantre
starter

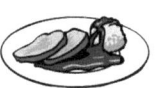

pla prinsipal
main course

deser
dessert

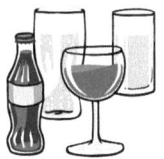

labwason
drinks

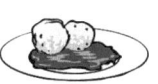

manze
food

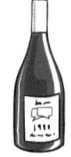

boutey
bottle

fast food
....
fast food

take-away
....
street food

teyer
....
teapot

po disik
....
sugar bowl

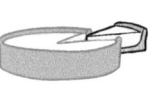

porsion
....
portion

masinn expresso
....
espresso machine

sez-ot
....
high chair

bill
....
bill

plato
....
tray

kouto
....
knife

fourset
....
fork

kwiyer
....
spoon

ti-kwiyer
....
teaspoon

serviet
....
serviette

ver
....
glass

lasiet
....
plate

lasiet
....
soup plate

soukoup
....
saucer

lasos
....
sauce

po disel
....
salt shaker

moulin dipwav
....
pepper mill

vineg
....
vinegar

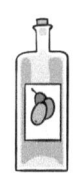

delwil
....
oil

zepis
....
spices

ketchup
....
ketchup

lamoutard
....
mustard

mayonez
....
mayonnaise

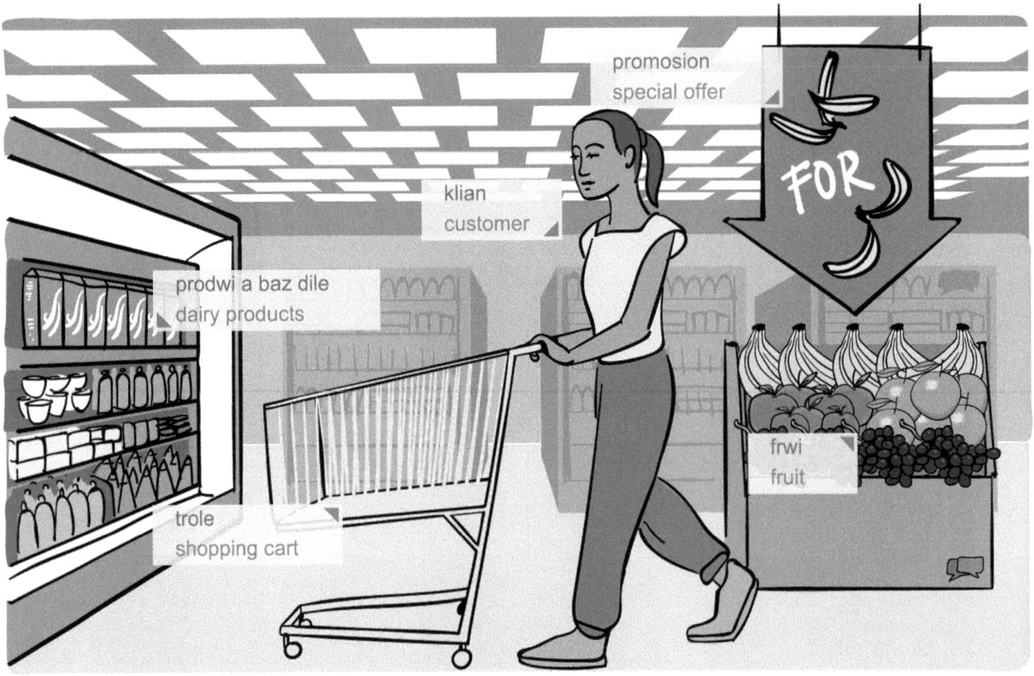

promosion
special offer

klian
customer

prodwi a baz dile
dairy products

FOR

frwi
fruit

trole
shopping cart

bousri	**boulanzri**	**peze**
butcher's shop	bakery	weigh
	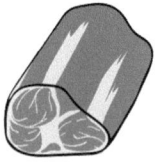	
legim	**laviann**	**aliman konzele**
vegetables	meat	frozen food

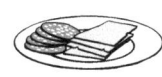

sarkitri

cold cuts

bwat konserv

canned food

lapoud masinn

detergent

bonbon

candy

komision

household products

deterzan

cleaning products

vandez

sales representative

lakes

cash register

kesie

cashier

lalis komision

shopping list

ouvertir

opening hours

portfey

wallet

kart kredi

credit card

sak

bag

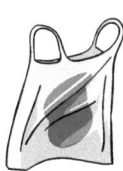

sak plastik

plastic bag

delo

water

zi

juice

dile

milk

coca

coke

divin

wine

labier

beer

lalkol

alcohol

sokola so

cocoa

dite

tea

kafe

coffee

expresso

espresso

cappuccino

cappuccino

banann

banana

pom

apple

zoranz

orange

melon

melon

sitron

lemon

karot

carrot

lay

garlic

banbou

bamboo

zwayon

onion

sanpiyon

mushroom

nwazet

nuts

minn

noodles

spageti

spaghetti

diri

rice

salad

salad

chips

fries

pomdeter frir

fried potatoes

pizza

pizza

burger

hamburger

sandwich

sandwich

eskalop

escalope

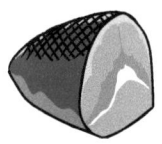

zanbon

ham

salami

salami

sosis

sausage

poul

chicken

roti

roast

pwason

fish

oatmeal
porridge oats

muesli
muesli

kornbif
cornflakes

lafarinn
flour

krwasan
croissant

ti-dipin
bread roll

dipin
bread

dipin griye
toast

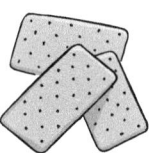

biskwi
cookies

diber
butter

fromaz blan
curd

gato
cake

dizef
egg

dizef frir
fried egg

fromaz
cheese

sorbe

ice cream

disik

sugar

dimiel

honey

konfitir

jelly

nouga

nougat cream

kari

curry

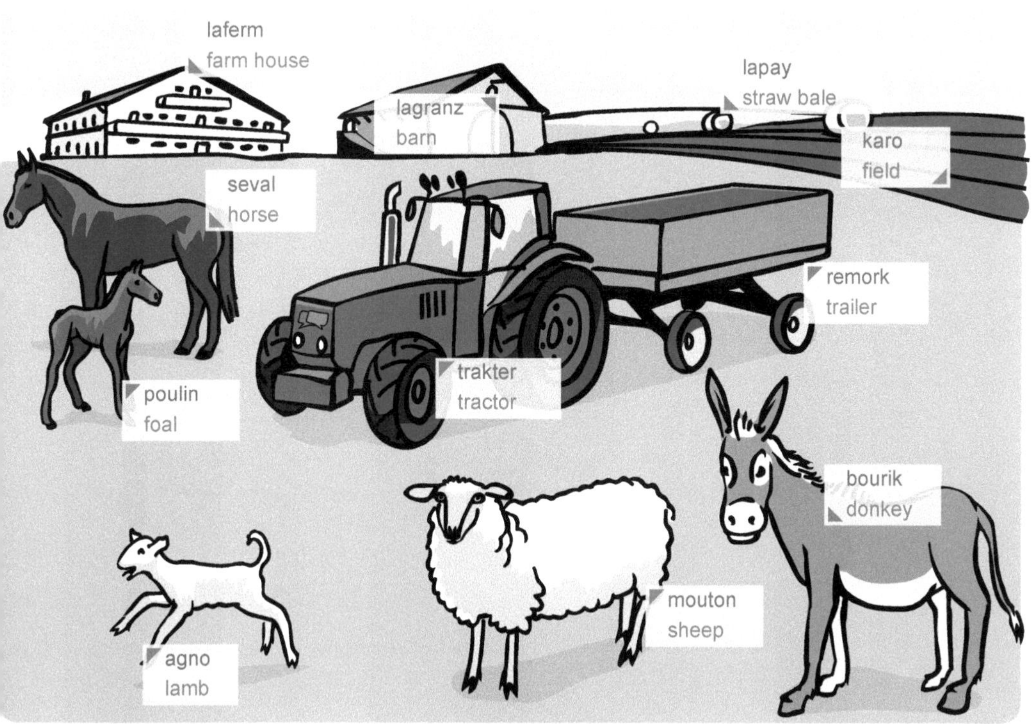

laferm
farm house

lagranz
barn

lapay
straw bale

karo
field

seval
horse

remork
trailer

poulin
foal

trakter
tractor

bourik
donkey

mouton
sheep

agno
lamb

kabri

goat

vas

cow

vo

calf

koson

pig

ti-koson

piglet

toro

bull

lezwa

goose

kanar

duck

pousin

chick

poul

hen

kok

cockerel

lera

rat

sat

cat

souri

mouse

bef

ox

lisien

dog

lakaz lisien

dog house

tiyo

garden hose

arozwar

watering can

laserp

scythe

saret

plow

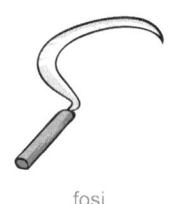

fosi

sickle

pios

hoe

fours

pitchfork

lars

axe

bouret

pushcart

kiv

trough

bwat dile

milk can

sak

sack

fencing

fence

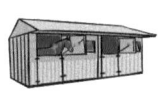

letab

stable

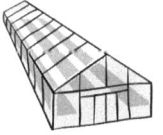

laser

greenhouse

later

soil

lagrin

seed

langre

fertilizer

masinn pou fer rekolt

combine harvester

rekolte

harvest

rekolt

harvest

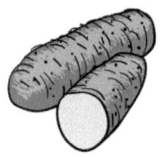

ignam

yams

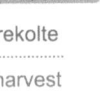

dible

wheat

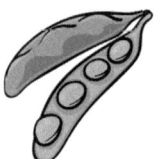

soya

soya

pomdeter

potato

may

corn

colza

rapeseed

zarb frwitie

fruit tree

maniok

manioc

sereal

grain

laferm - farm

lakaz

house

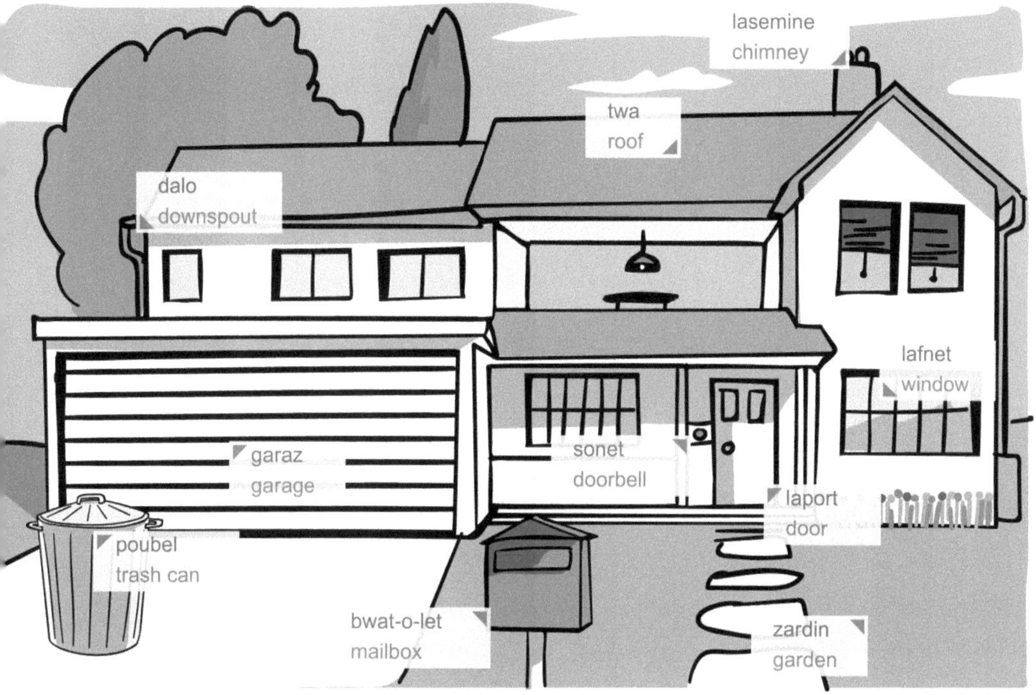
lasemine
chimney
twa
roof
dalo
downspout
lafnet
window
garaz
garage
sonet
doorbell
laport
door
poubel
trash can
bwat-o-let
mailbox
zardin
garden

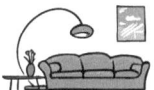

salon

living room

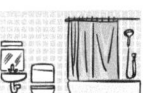

saldebin

bathroom

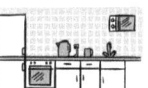

lakwizinn

kitchen

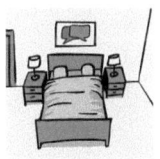

lasam

bedroom

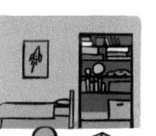

lasam zanfan

kids room

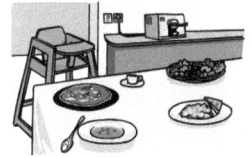

salamanze

dining room

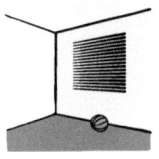

sali
floor

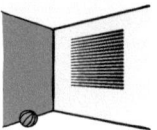

miray
wall

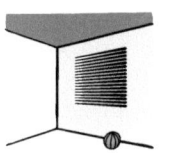

plafon
ceiling

lakav
cellar

sona
sauna

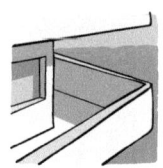

balkon
balcony

teras
terrace

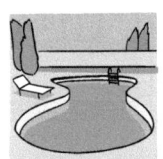

pisinn
pool

masinn koup gazon
lawn mower

dra
sheet

kwet
bedspread

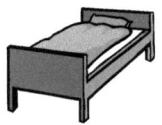

lili
bed

balie
broom

seo
bucket

take lalimier
switch

salon

living room

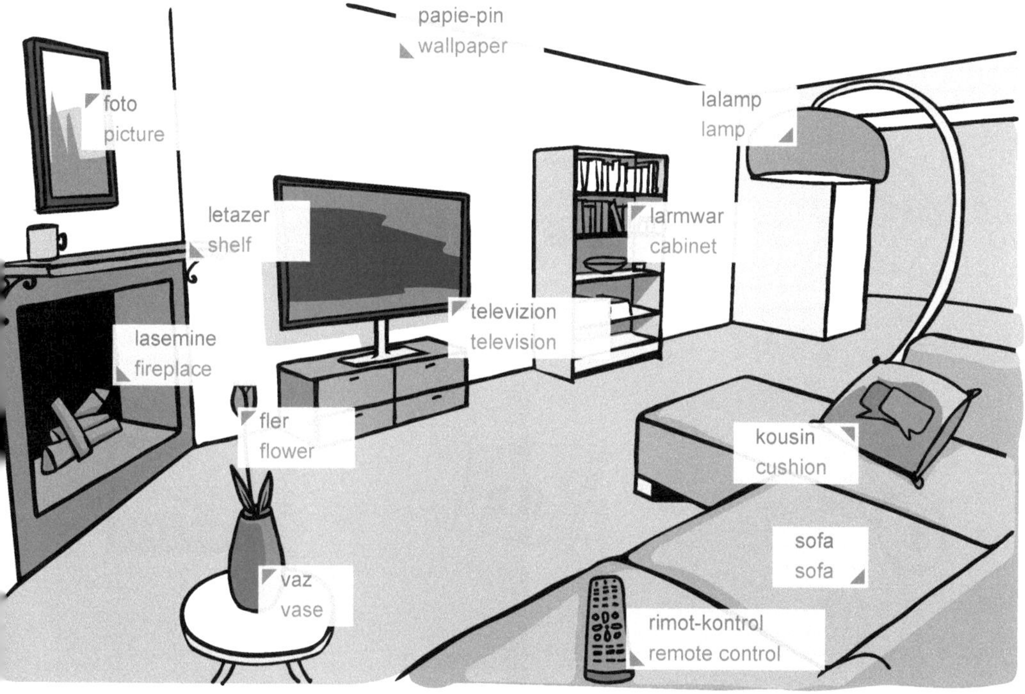

papie-pin
wallpaper
foto
picture
lalamp
lamp
letazer
shelf
larmwar
cabinet
televizion
television
lasemine
fireplace
fler
flower
kousin
cushion
sofa
sofa
vaz
vase
rimot-kontrol
remote control

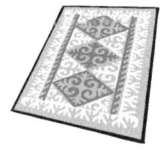

tapi

carpet

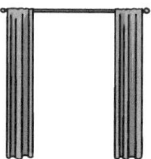

rido

drape

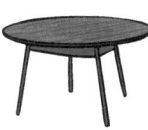

latab

table

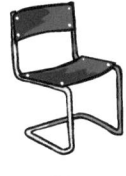

sez

chair

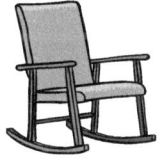

rocking chair

rocking chair

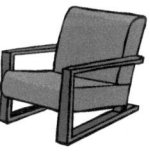

fotey

armchair

liv

book

kouvertir

blanket

dekorasion

decoration

dibwa foye

firewood

fim

film

hi-fi

stereo system

lakle

key

zournal

newspaper

lapintir

painting

poster

poster

radio

radio

bloknot

notebook

laspirater

vacuum cleaner

kaktis

cactus

labouzi

candle

lakwizinn
kitchen

frizider
fridge
mikro-ond
microwave oven
balans
kitchen scales
toaster
toaster
deterzan
laundry detergent
four
stove
frizer
freezer
poubel
trash can
lav-vesel
dishwasher

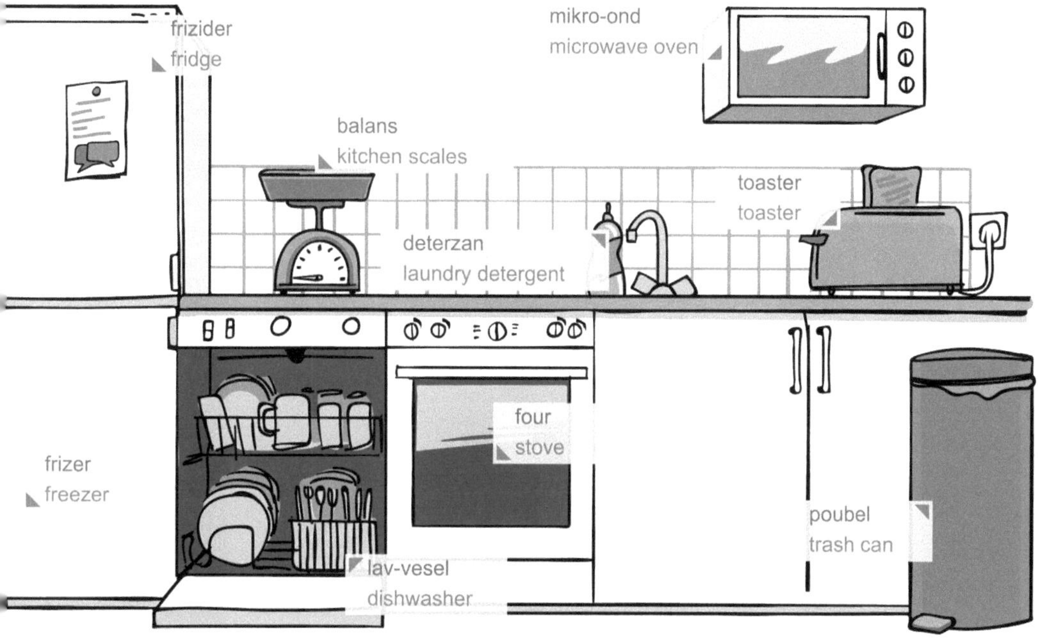

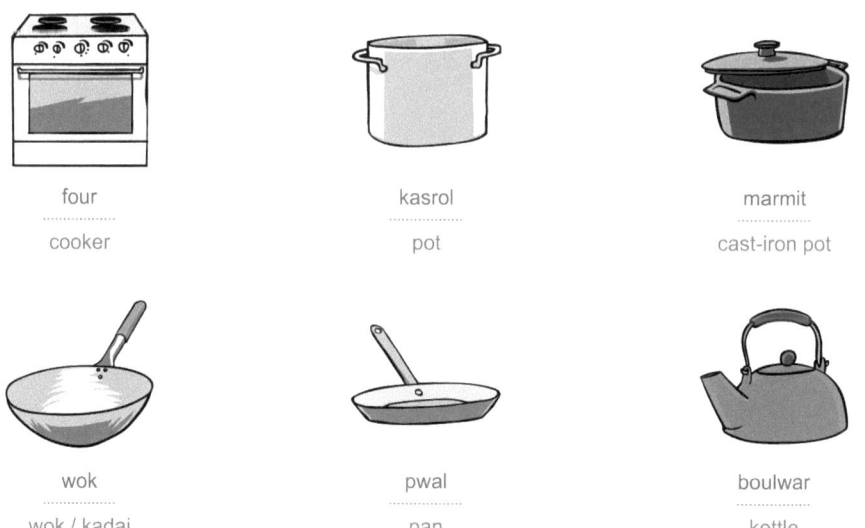

four

cooker

kasrol

pot

marmit

cast-iron pot

wok

wok / kadai

pwal

pan

boulwar

kettle

steamer

steamer

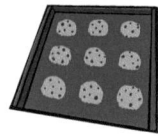

plak kwison

baking tray

vesel

crockery

goble

mug

bol

bowl

baget sinwa

chopsticks

lous

ladle

spatil

spatula

fwet

whisk

paswar

strainer

tami

sieve

larap

grater

mortie

mortar

griyad

barbecue

lasemine

fireplace

biyo

chopping board

roulo

rolling pin

tirbouson

corkscrew

bwat konserv

can

ouvbwat

can opener

legan proteksion

oven cloth

lavabo

sink

bros

brush

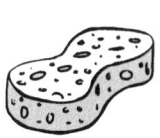

leponz

sponge

blender

blender

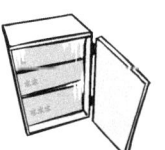

konzelater

deep freezer

bibron

baby bottle

robine

tap

saldebin

bathroom

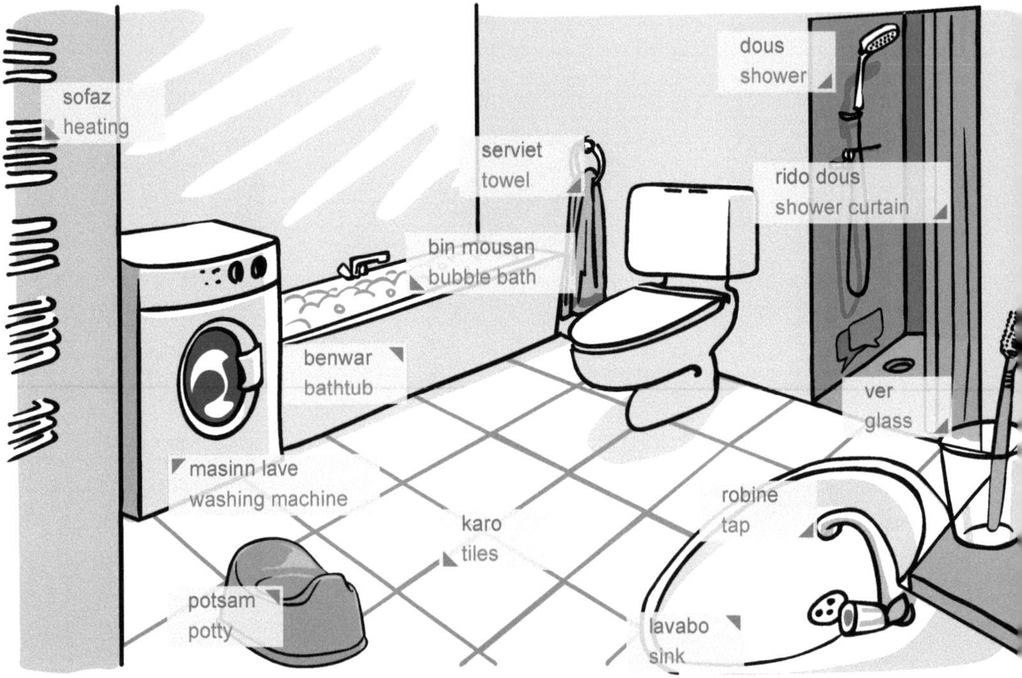

sofaz
heating

dous
shower

serviet
towel

rido dous
shower curtain

bin mousan
bubble bath

benwar
bathtub

ver
glass

masinn lave
washing machine

karo
tiles

robine
tap

potsam
potty

lavabo
sink

twalet
....
toilet

twalet
....
squat toilet

bide
....
bidet

piswar
....
urinal

papie twalet
....
toilet paper

bros twalet
....
toilet brush

bros ledan

toothbrush

dantifris

toothpaste

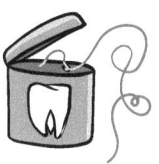

fil danter

dental floss

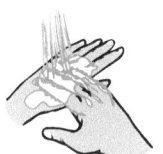

lave

wash

ti-bin

hand shower

dous

douche

basin

basin

bros ledo

back brush

savon

soap

zel dous

shower gel

sanpwin

shampoo

gandebin

flannel

drin

drain

lakrem

creme

deodoran

deodorant

mirwar

mirror

mirwar

hand mirror

razwar

razor

lamous pou raze

shaving foam

apre-razaz

aftershave

pengn

comb

bros

brush

seswar

hair-dryer

lak

hairspray

makiyaz

makeup

dirouz

lipstick

verni

nail varnish

cotton wool

cotton wool

tay-zong

nail scissors

parfin

perfume

trous twalet

washbag

stoul

stool

balans

weighing scales

penwar

bathrobe

legan netwayaz

rubber gloves

tanpon

tampon

serviet izienik

sanitary towel

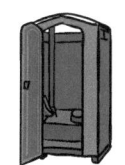

twalet simik

chemical toilet

lasam zanfan

kids room

revey
alarm clock
doudou
cuddly toy
ti loto
toy car
ose
rattle
lakaz zouzou
doll's house
kado
present

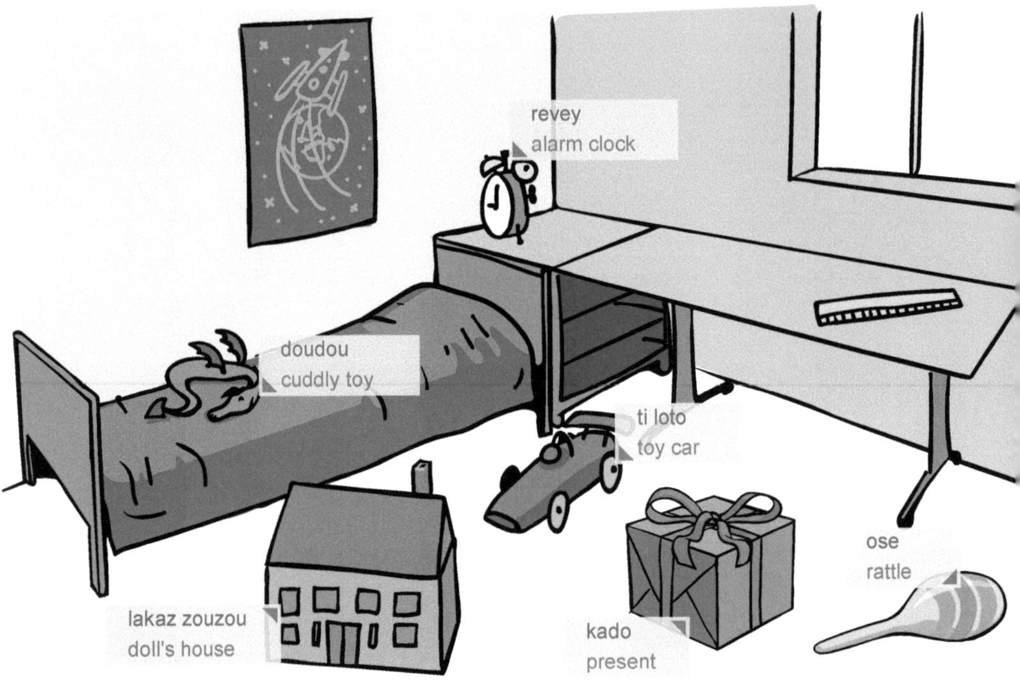

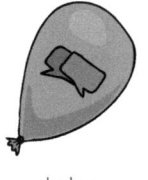

balon

balloon

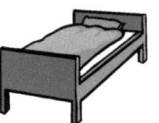

lili

bed

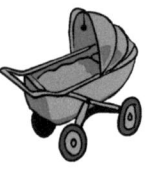

pouset

stroller

kart

deck of cards

puzzle

jigsaw

SUPER
MEGA

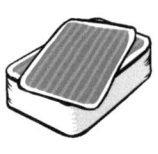

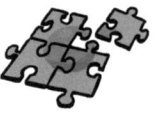

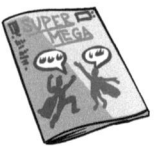

tikomik

comic

lego
....
lego bricks

lego
....
toy blocks

figirinn
....
action figure

grenouyer
....
romper suit

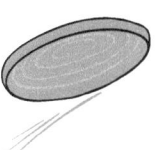

frisbee
....
frisbee

mobil
....
mobile

zwe
....
board game

lede
....
dice

trin zouzou
....
model train set

siset
....
pacifier

fet
....
party

liv ek zimaz
....
picture book

boul
....
ball

poupet
....
doll

zwe
....
play

bak-a-sab
....
sandpit

balanswar
....
swing

zouzou
....
toys

game
....
video game console

trisik
....
tricycle

nounours
....
teddy bear

larmwar
....
wardrobe

linz

clothing

soset
....
socks

leba
....
stockings

kolan
....
tights

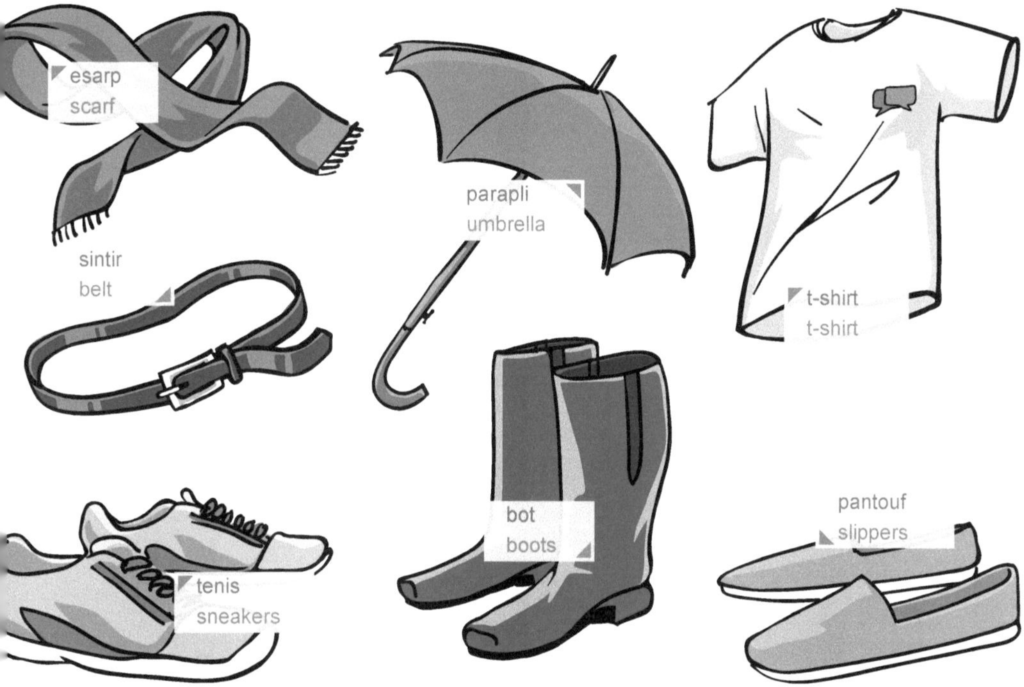

esarp
scarf

parapli
umbrella

t-shirt
t-shirt

sintir
belt

bot
boots

pantouf
slippers

tenis
sneakers

sandalet
sandals

soulie
shoes

bot an karotsou
rubber boots

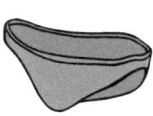

souvetman
underwear

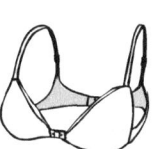

soutiengorz
bra

vest
undershirt

body

body

pantalon

pants

jeans

jeans

zip

skirt

blouz

blouse

simiz

shirt

pull-over

pullover

blouzon ek kapison

sweater

vest

blazer

jaket

jacket

manto

coat

pardesi

raincoat

kostim

costume

rob

dress

rob lamarye

wedding dress

kostim

suit

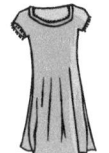

robdesam

nightgown

pizama

pajamas

sari

sari

foular

headscarf

tirban

turban

bourka

burka

kaftan

kaftan

abaya

abaya

mayo de bin

swimsuit

mayo de bin

trunks

sorti de sekour

shorts

linz spor

tracksuit

tabliye

apron

legan

gloves

bouton

button

linet

glasses

brasle

bracelet

kolie

necklace

bag

ring

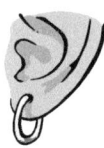

zanon

earring

bone

cap

sint

coat hanger

sapo

hat

kravat

tie

fermetirekler

zip

elmet

helmet

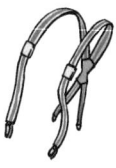

bretel

braces

iniform lekol

school uniform

iniform

uniform

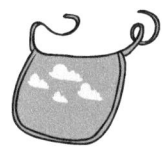

bavwar

bib

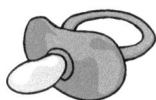

siset

pacifier

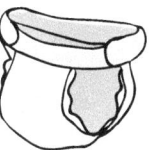

lanz

diaper

biro

office

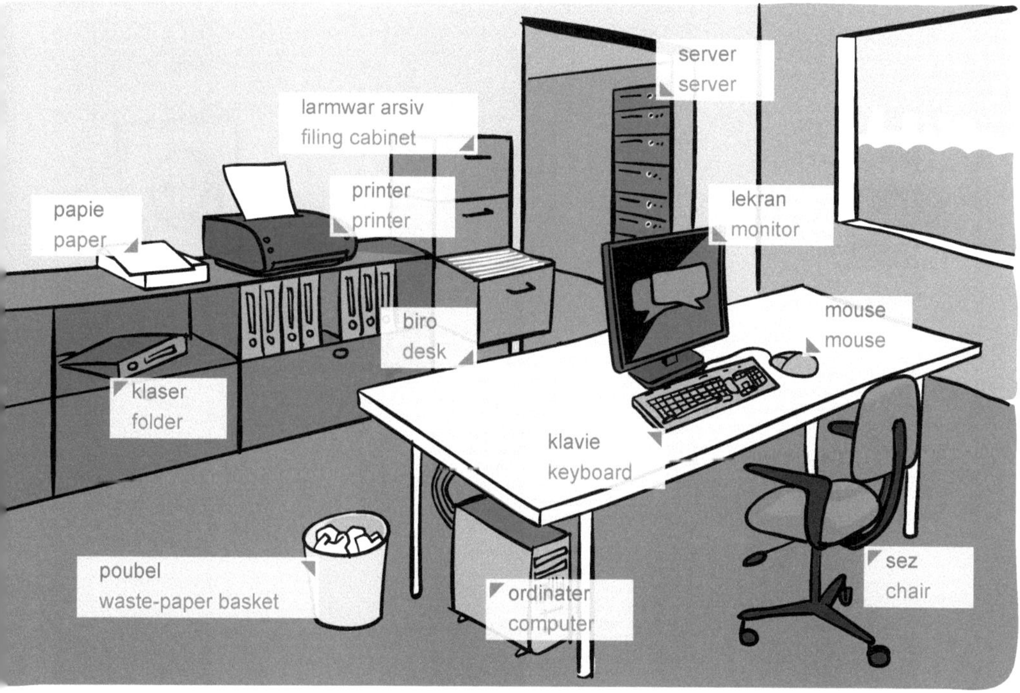
server
server
larmwar arsiv
filing cabinet
printer
printer
papie
paper
lekran
monitor
mouse
mouse
biro
desk
klaser
folder
klavie
keyboard
poubel
waste-paper basket
ordinater
computer
sez
chair

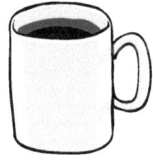

mug

coffee mug

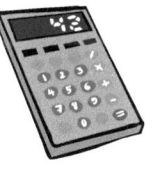

kalkilatris

calculator

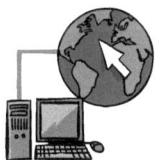

internet

internet

laptop
laptop

let
letter

mesaz
message

portab
cell phone

rezo
network

fotokopi
photocopier

lozisiel
software

telefonn
telephone

priz
plug socket

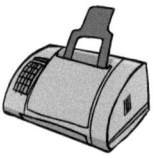

fax
fax machine

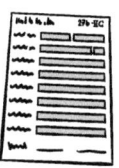

form
form

dokiman
document

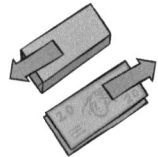

aste

buy

peye

pay

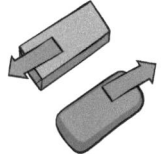

fer biznes

trade

larzan

money

dolar

dollar

euro

euro

yen

yen

rouble

rouble

fran swis

Swiss franc

renminbi yuan

renminbi yuan

roupi

rupee

distribiter biye

cash point

biro sanz

currency exchange office

lor

gold

larzan

silver

petrol

oil

lenerzi

energy

pri

price

kontra

contract

tax

tax

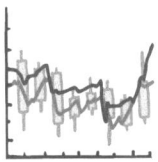

aksion

stock

travay

work

anplwaye

employee

anplwayer

employer

lizinn

factory

magazin

shop

travay
occupations

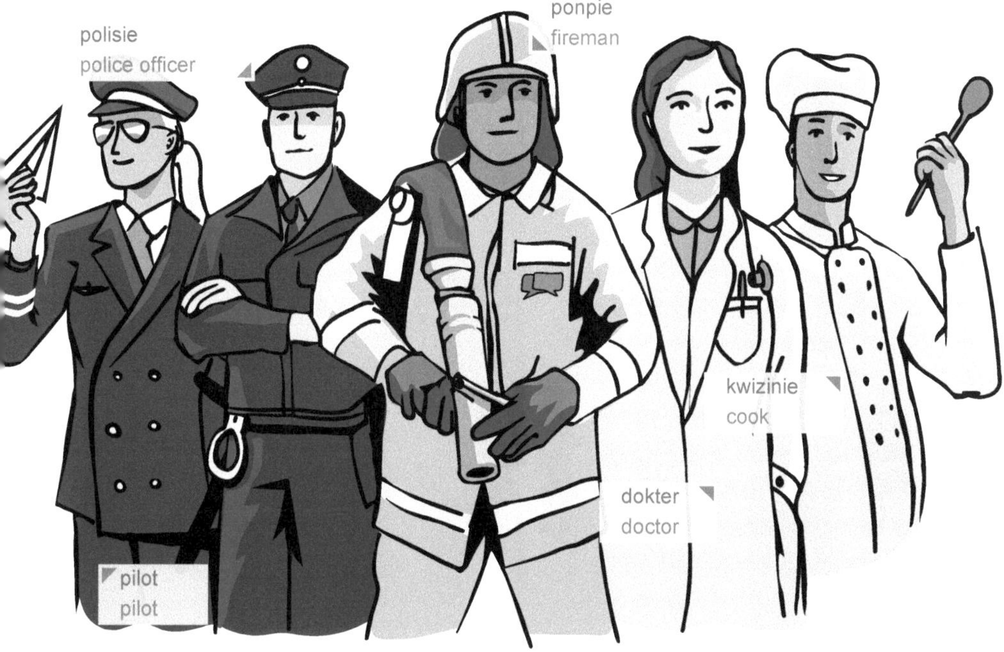

polisie
police officer
ponpie
fireman
kwizinie
cook
dokter
doctor
pilot
pilot

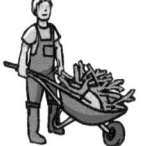

zardinie

gardener

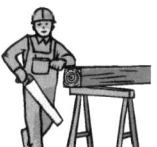

sarpantie

carpenter

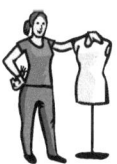

koutirier

seamstress

ziz

judge

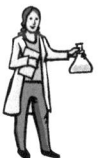

simis

chemist

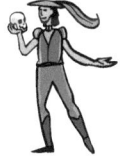

akter

actor

sofer bis

bus driver

sofer taxi

taxi driver

peser

fisherman

bonn

cleaning lady

zouvriye twa lakaz

roofer

server

waiter

saser

hunter

pint

painter

boulanze

baker

elektrisien

electrician

zouvriye

builder

inzenier

engineer

bouse

butcher

plonbie

plumber

fakter

postman

solda

soldier

arsitek

architect

kesie

cashier

fleris

florist

kwafez

hairdresser

chek

conductor

mekanisien

mechanic

kapitenn

captain

dantis

dentist

siantis

scientist

rabi

rabbi

imam

imam

mwann

monk

pret

pastor

zouti
tools

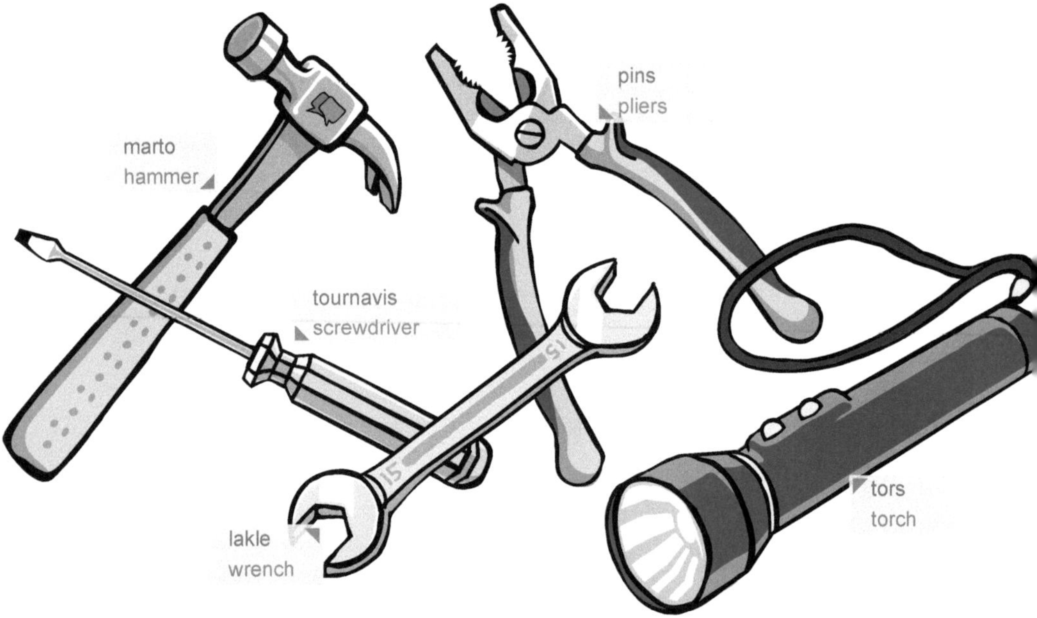
marto
hammer
pins
pliers
tournavis
screwdriver
lakle
wrench
tors
torch

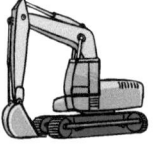

peltez

excavator

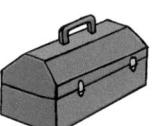

bwat zouti

toolbox

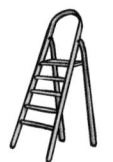

lesel

ladder

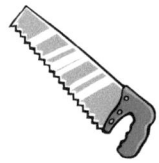

lasi

saw

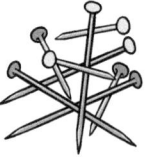

koulou

nails

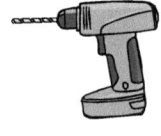

persez

drill

aranze

repair

lapel

shovel

Ayo!

Damn!

lapel

dustpan

po lapintir

paint can

vis

screws

instriman lamizik
musical instruments

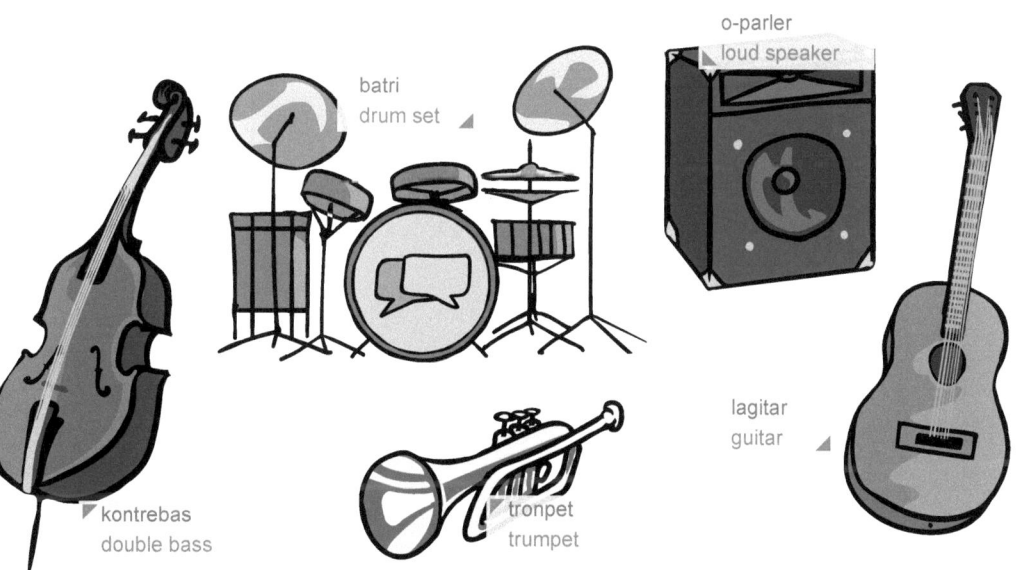

o-parler
loud speaker

batri
drum set

lagitar
guitar

kontrebas
double bass

tronpet
trumpet

piano

piano

violon

violin

bas

bass

tinbal

timpani

tanbour

drums

klavie

keyboard

saxofonn

saxophone

laflit

flute

mikro

microphone

instriman lamizik - musical instruments

ZOO

tig
tiger

lantre
entrance

kaz
cage

zeb
zebra

manze pou zanimo
animal feed

panda
panda

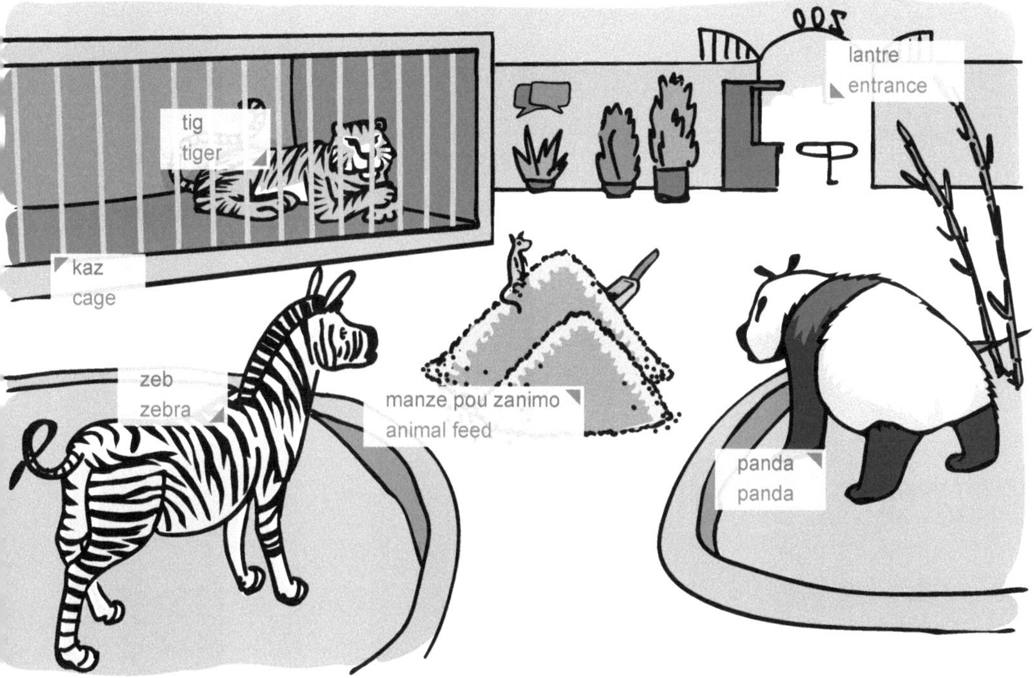

zanimo

animals

lelefan

elephant

kangourou

kangaroo

rinoceros

rhino

gori

gorilla

lours

bear

samo

camel

lotris

ostrich

lion

lion

zako

monkey

flaman roz

flamingo

peroke

parrot

lours poler

polar bear

pingwi

penguin

rekin

shark

pan

peacock

serpan

snake

krokodil

crocodile

gardien zoo

zookeeper

fok

seal

zagwar

jaguar

poney

pony

leopar

leopard

ipopotam

hippo

ziraf

giraffe

leg

eagle

sangliye

boar

pwason

fish

torti

turtle

mors

walrus

renar

fox

gazel

gazelle

foutborl ameriken
American football

siklism
cycling

tenis
tennis

basketball
basketball

natasion
swimming

oke lor gazon
ice hockey

labox
boxing

foutborl
soccer

badminton
badminton

atletism
athletics

handball
handball

ski
skiing

polo
polo

sote
jump

riye
laugh

maye
hug

marse
walk

sante
sing

reve
dream

priye
pray

anbrase
kiss

ekrir
write

desine
draw

montre
show

pouse
push

done
give

pran
take

ena

have

fer

do

ete

be

diboute

stand

galoupe

run

rise

pull

zete

throw

tonbe

fall

alonze

lie

atann

wait

amene

carry

asize

sit

abiye

get dressed

dormi

sleep

leve

wake up

gete

look at

plore

cry

karese

stroke

pengne

comb

koze

talk

konpran

understand

dimande

ask

ekoute

listen

bwar

drink

manze

eat

netwaye

tidy up

kontan

love

kwi

cook

kondir

drive

anvole

fly

aktivite - activities

fer lavwal
....
sail

kalkile
....
calculate

lir
....
read

aprann
....
learn

travay
....
work

marye
....
marry

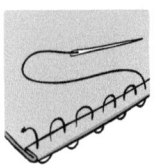

koud
....
sew

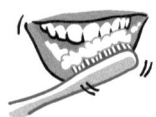

bros ledan
....
brush teeth

touye
....
kill

fime
....
smoke

avoye
....
send

fami

family

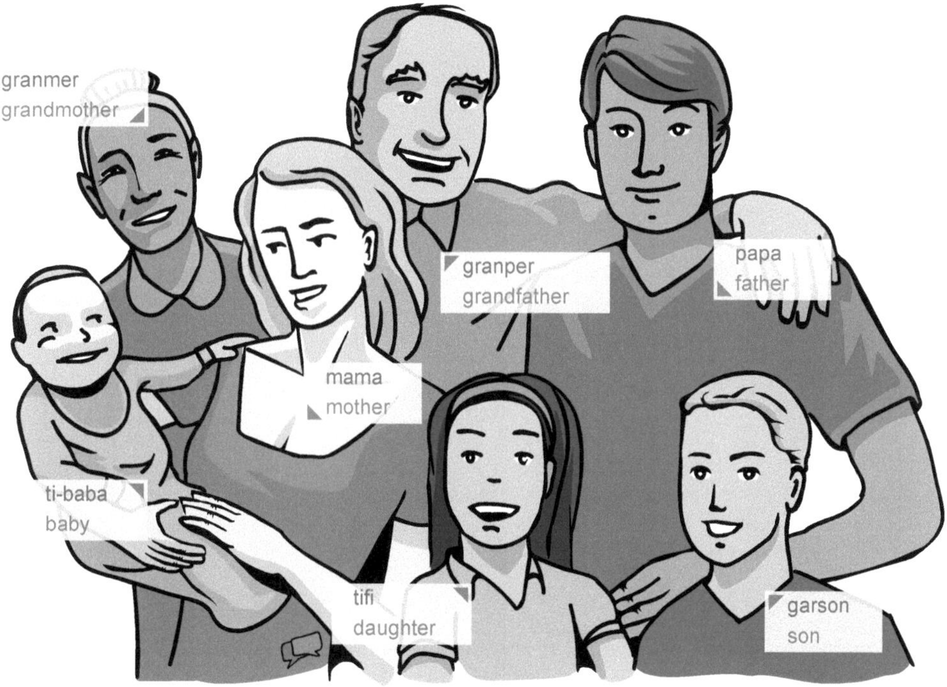

granmer
grandmother
granper
grandfather
papa
father
mama
mother
ti-baba
baby
tifi
daughter
garson
son

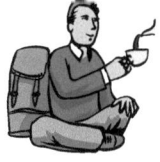

ot

guest

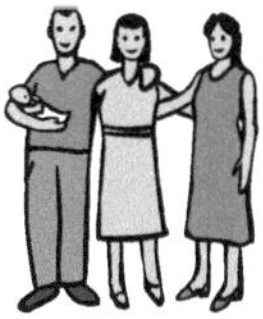

matant

aunt

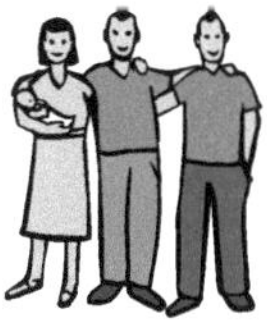

tonton

uncle

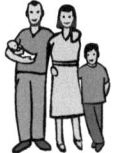

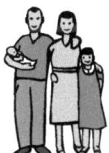

frer

brother

ser

sister

lekor

body

fron
forehead
lizie
eye
zepol
shoulder
ledwa
finger
figir
face
manton
chin
lame
hand
lazam
leg
tete
breast
lebra
arm

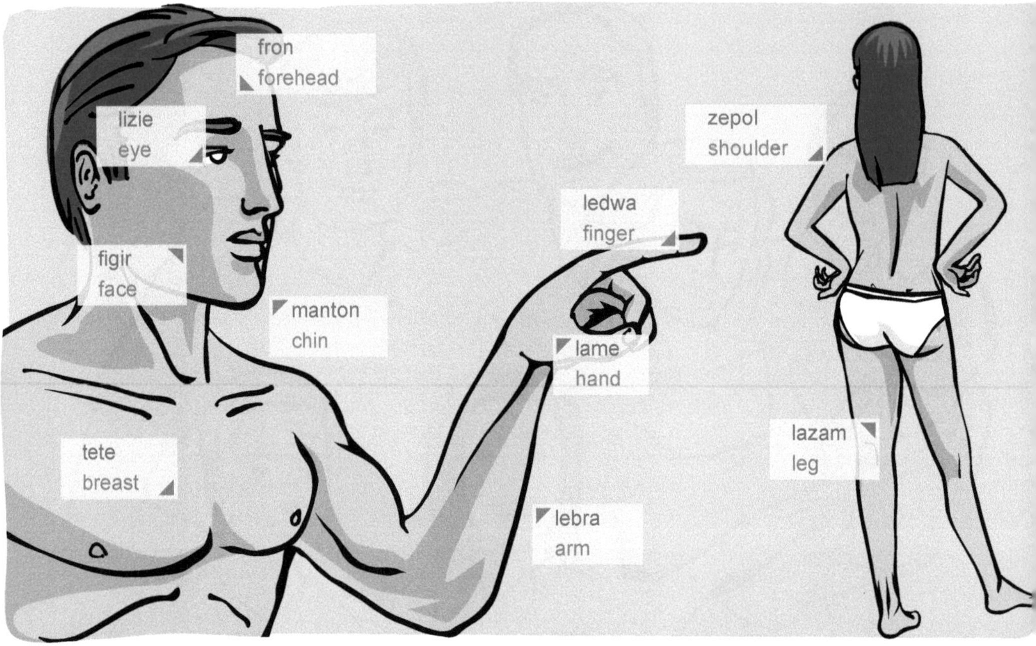

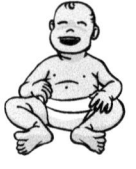

ti-baba

baby

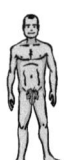

zom

man

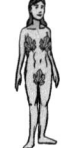

fam

woman

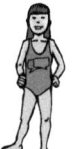

tifi

girl

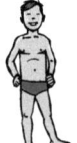

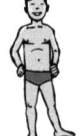

ti-garson

boy

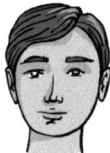

latet

head

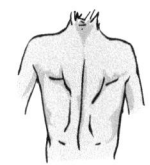

ledo

back

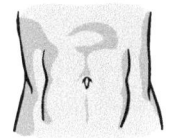

vant

belly

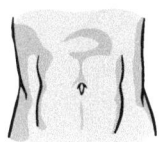

lonbri

navel

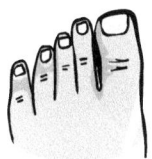

zortey

toe

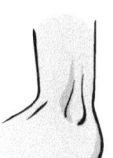

talon

heel

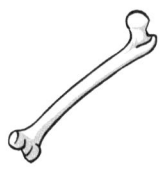

lezo

bone

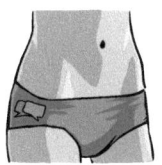

laans

hip

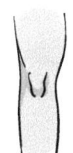

zenou

knee

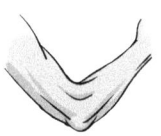

koud

elbow

nene

nose

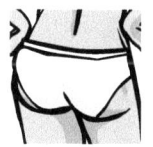

fes

buttocks

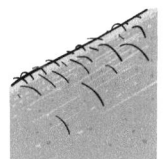

lapo

skin

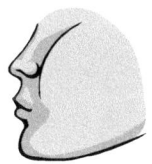

lazou

cheek

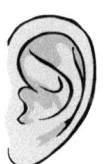

zorey

ear

lalev

lip

labous

mouth

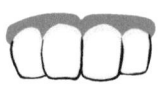

ledan

tooth

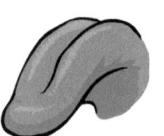

lalang

tongue

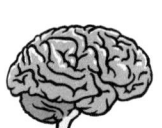

servo

brain

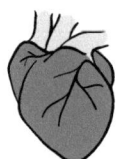

leker

heart

mix

muscle

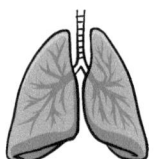

poumon

lung

lefwa

liver

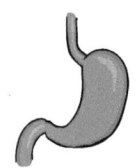

lestoma

stomach

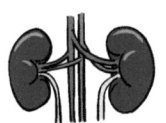

lerin

kidneys

sex

sex

kapot

condom

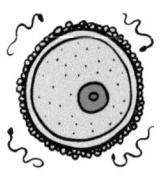

ovil

ovum

sperm

semen

groses

pregnancy

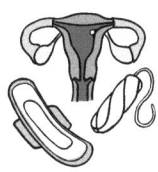

period
menstruation

vazin
vagina

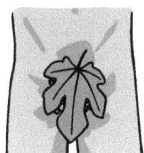

penis
penis

soursi
eyebrow

seve
hair

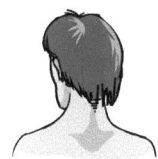

likou
neck

lopital
hospital

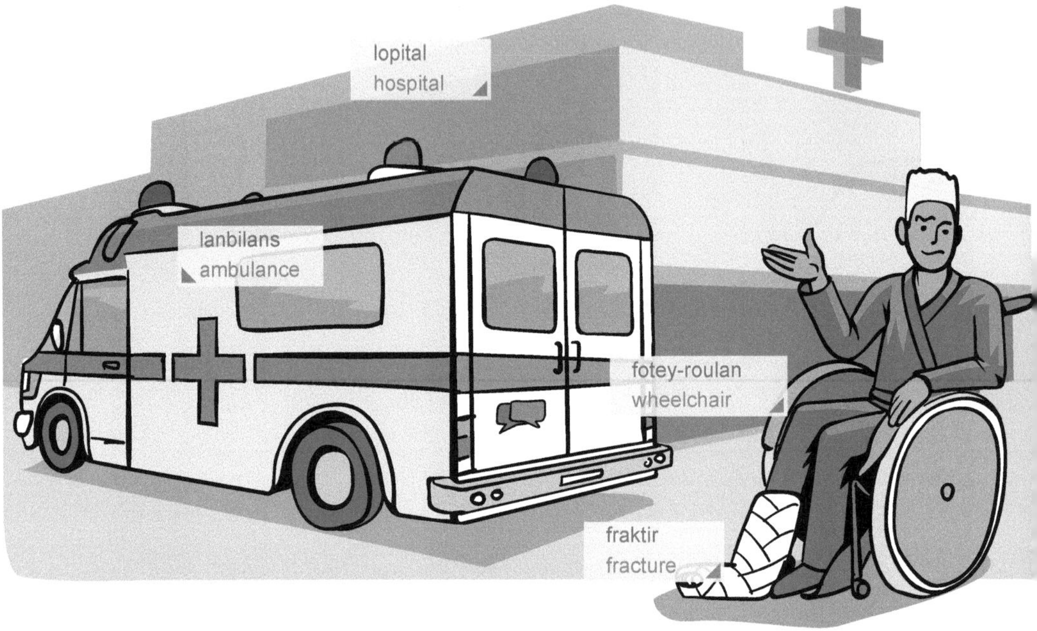

lopital
hospital
lanbilans
ambulance
fotey-roulan
wheelchair
fraktir
fracture

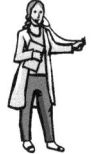

dokter

doctor

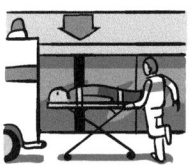

servis irzans

emergency room

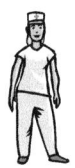

ners

nurse

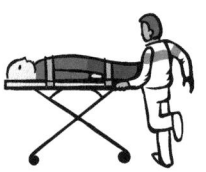

irzans

emergency

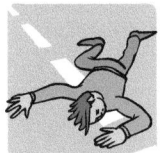

inkonsian

unconscious

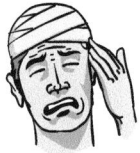

douler

pain

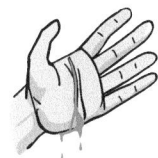

blesir
injury

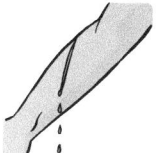

emorazi
bleeding

kriz kardiak
heart attack

atak serebral
stroke

alerzik
allergy

touse
cough

lafiev
fever

lagrip
flu

diare
diarrhea

malad latet
headache

kanser
cancer

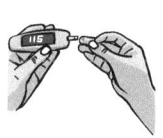

diabet
diabetes

sirirzien
surgeon

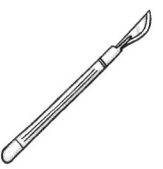

skalpel
scalpel

operasion
operation

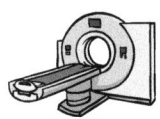

CT

CT

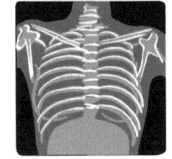

x-ray

x-ray

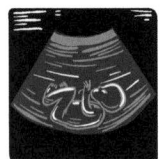

iltrason

ultrasound

mask

face mask

maladi

disease

sal-datant

waiting room

beki

crutch

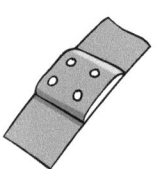

pansman

plaster

bandaz

bandage

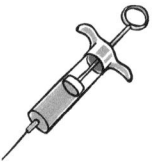

inzeksion

injection

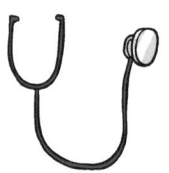

stetoskop

stethoscope

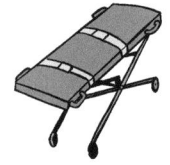

brankar

stretcher

termomet

clinical thermometer

nesans

birth

sirpwa

overweight

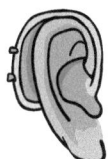

laparey oditif

hearing aid

dezinfektan

disinfectant

infeksion

infection

viris

virus

HIV / SIDA

HIV / AIDS

medsinn

medicine

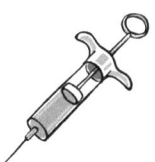

vaksinasion

vaccination

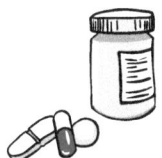

konprime

tablets

pilil kontraseptif

pill

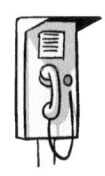

korl irzans

emergency call

laparey tansion

blood pressure monitor

malad / bien

ill / healthy

o-sekour

Help!

alarm

alarm

atak

assault

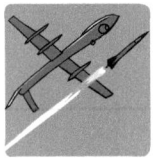

atak

attack

danze

danger

sorti de sekour

emergency exit

Dife!

Fire!

laponp dife

fire extinguisher

aksidan

accident

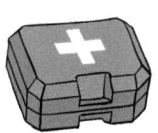

kit first aid

first-aid kit

SOS

SOS

lapolis

police

lerop

Europe

Lamerik di nor

North America

Lamerik di sid

South America

lafrik

Africa

lazi

Asia

lostrali

Australia

latlantik

Atlantic

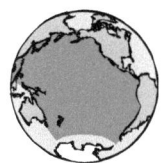

pasifik

Pacific

losean indien

Indian Ocean

losean antartik

Antarctic Ocean

losean artik

Arctic Ocean

Pol Nor

North pole

Pol Sid

South pole

lantartik

Antarctica

later

earth

later

land

lamer

sea

zil

island

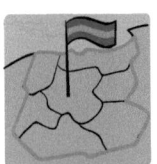

nasion

nation

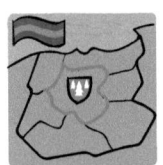

leta

state

kadran

clock face

zegwi ler

hour hand

zegwi minit

minute hand

zegwi segonn

second hand

ki ler la ?

What time is it?

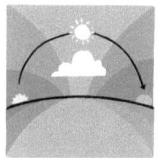

zour

day

lctan

time

aster-la

now

mont dizital

digital watch

minit

minute

ler

hour

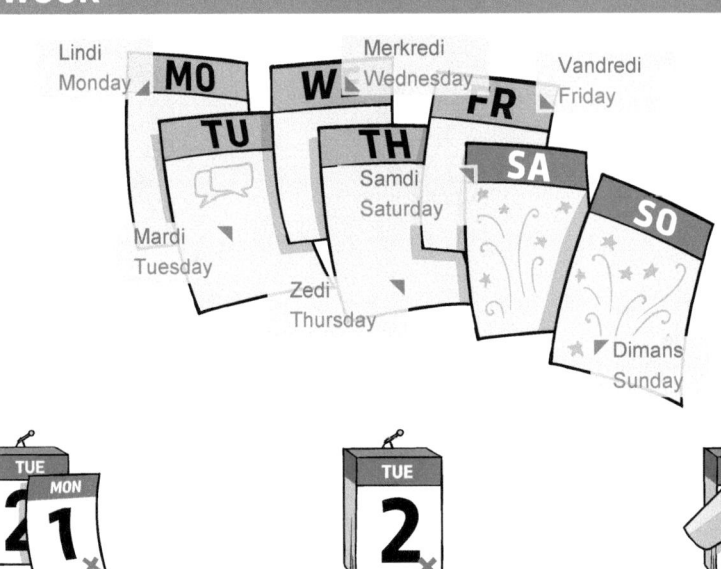

Lindi / Monday
Merkredi / Wednesday
Vandredi / Friday
Mardi / Tuesday
Zedi / Thursday
Samdi / Saturday
Dimans / Sunday

yer

yesterday

zordi

today

demin

tomorrow

gramatin

morning

midi

noon

aswar

evening

zour travay

workdays

wikenn

weekend

lapli
rain

larkansiel
rainbow

lanez
snow

divan[
wind

printan
spring

otonn
fall

lete
summer

liver
winter

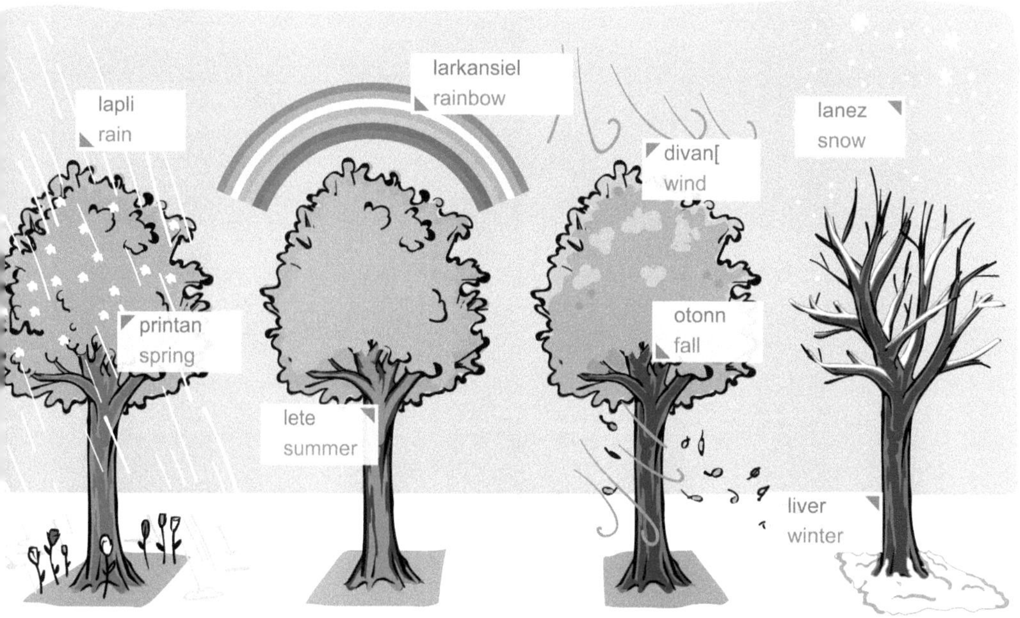

meteo

weather forecast

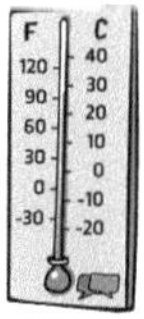

termomet

thermometer

lalimier soley

sunshine

niaz

cloud

brouyar

fog

limidite

humidity

lafoud

lightning

toner

thunder

tanpet

storm

lagrel

hail

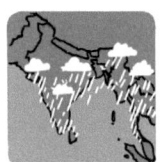

mouson

monsoon

inondasion

flood

laglas

ice

Zanvie

January

Fevriye

February

Mars

March

Avril

April

Me

May

Zien

June

Zilie

July

Out

August

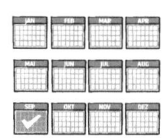

Septam

September

Oktob

October

Novam

November

Desam

December

form

shapes

ron

circle

kare

square

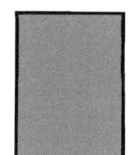

rektang

rectangle

triang

triangle

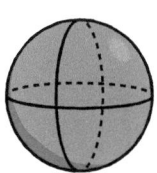

sfer

sphere

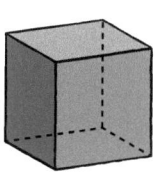

kib

cube

blan

white

zonn

yellow

oranz

orange

roz

pink

rouz

red

mov

purple

ble

blue

ver

green

maron

brown

gri

gray

nwar

black

boukou / enn tigit

a lot / a little

ankoler / kalm

angry / calm

zoli / vilin

beautiful / ugly

koumansman / lafin

beginning / end

gro / tipti

big / small

kler / obskirite

bright / dark

frer / ser

brother / sister

prop / sal

clean / dirty

konple / inkonple

complete / incomplete

lizour / lanwit

day / night

vivan / mor

dead / alive

larz / sere

wide / narrow

komestib / inkomestib

edible / inedible

move / bon

evil / kind

exsite / agase

excited / bored

gra / mins

fat / thin

premie / dernie

first / last

kamwad / lennmi

friend / enemy

ranpli / vid

full / empty

dir / mou

hard / soft

lour / leze

heavy / light

fin / swaf

hunger / thirst

malad / bien

ill / healthy

ilegal / legal

illegal / legal

intelizan / kouyon

intelligent / stupid

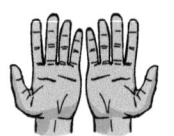

gos / drwat

left / right

pre / lwin

near / far

nouvo / ize

new / used

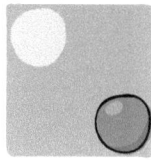

nanye / kiksoz

nothing / something

vie / zenn

old / young

demare / arete

on / off

ouver / ferme

open / closed

trankil / for

quiet / loud

ris / pov

rich / poor

bon / move

right / wrong

brit / lis

rough / smooth

tris / zwaye

sad / happy

kourt / long

short / long

lan / rapid

slow / fast

tranpe / sek

wet / dry

so / fre

warm / cool

lager / lape

war / peace

numbers

0

zero

zero

1

enn

one

2

de

two

3

trwa

three

4

kat

four

5

sink

five

6

sis

six

7

set

seven

8

wit

eight

9

nef

nine

10

distribiter biye

ten

11

onz

eleven

12

douz

twelve

13

trez

thirteen

14

katorz

fourteen

15

kinz

fifteen

16

sez

sixteen

17

diset

seventeen

18

dizwit

eighteen

19

diznef

nineteen

20

vin

twenty

100

san

hundred

1.000

mil

thousand

1.000.000

milyon

million

Angle

English

Angle Lamerik

American English

Mandarin Sinwa

Chinese Mandarin

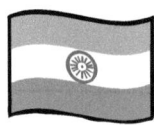

Hindi

Hindi

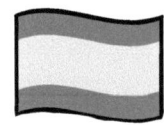

espagnol

Spanish

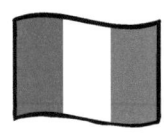

Franse

French

Arab

Arabic

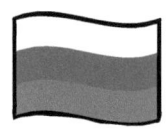

Ris

Russian

Portige

Portuguese

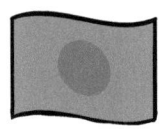

Bengali

Bengali

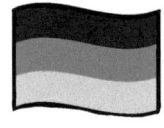

Alman

German

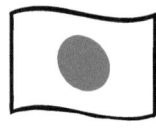

Zapone

Japanese

mo

I

to

you

li

he / she / it

nou

we

ou

you

zot

they

kisana?

who?

kiete?

what?

kouma?

how?

kotsa?

where?

kan?

when?

nom

name

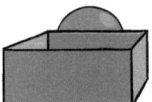

deryer

behind

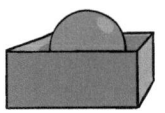

dan

in

devan

in front of

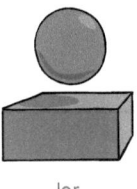

lor

over

lor

on

anba

under

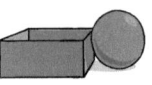

akote

beside

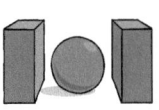

ant

between

plas

place